New Salad Cookbook

Ideals Publishing Corporation
Nashville, Tennessee

Contents

Fancy Fruit Salads 4

Seafood Specials 12

Pasta Pleasers 19

Main Dish Salads 24

Tempting Tosses 33

Zesty Marinades 44

Molded Salads 52

Dressings 59

Index 64

Published by Ideals Publishing Corporation
Nelson Place at Elm Hill Pike
Nashville, Tennessee

This book is one of a series of cookbooks including the following titles:

Budget Saving Meals Cookbook   *30-Minute Meals Cookbook*
Chicken and Poultry Cookbook   *All Holidays Menus Cookbook*
Grill and Barbecue Cooking   *American Regional Cookbook*
Ground Meat Cookbook   *Boys & Girls Cookbook*
Guide to Microwave Cookbook   *Christmas Cookbook*
Hershey's Chocolate and Cocoa Cookbook *Country Baking Cookbook*
Low Calorie Cookbook   *Fish and Seafood Cookbook*
Lunch and Brunch Cookbook   *Light & Delicious Cookbook*
Old-Fashioned Family Cookbook   *Casseroles & One Dish Meals*
Soup, Salad and Sandwich Cookbook   *New Salad Cookbook*
Quick & Simple Cooking for Two   *Wok Cookbook*

These and other Ideals books are available in a SOFTCOVER edition in bulk quantities at quantity discount for fund-raising or premium use. For information, please write SPECIAL SALES DEPARTMENT, Ideals Publishing Corporation, P.O. Box 140300, Nashville, TN 37214

The HARDCOVER edition of selected Titles is published in a limited edition for the exclusive use of Wayne Matthews Corporation, P.O. Box 54, Safety Harbor, FL 34695.

Cover Photo:
Mexican Salad, 25;
Sunny Salsa Salad, 39;
Corn Relish, 46

Photographs on pages 7, 23, 34, and 47 courtesy Dole ®
Photographs on pages 14, 26, 30, and 50 courtesy Pepperidge Farm ®

Fancy Fruit Salads

Homemade Applesauce

Makes 6 servings

2½ pounds apples
Sugar
Cinnamon

Wash apples and cut into quarters; peel and core. Place in saucepan with enough water to cover. Bring to a boil; reduce heat and simmer until tender (8 to 10 minutes). Mash with a potato masher. Add sugar to taste and cook over low heat for 3 more minutes. Serve with a sprinkle of cinnamon.

Grape Cup

Makes 4 servings

¼ cup orange juice
2 tablespoons orange liqueur
½ cup seedless green grapes
½ cup seedless red grapes
½ cup grapefruit segments
½ cup cubed melon
½ cup sliced banana
4 small grape clusters

Combine orange juice and liqueur in medium-sized bowl. Stir in grapes, grapefruit, melon, and banana. Chill for 1 hour. To serve, divide fruit into 4 servings and place in fruit cups. Garnish with grape clusters.

Ambrosia

Makes 8 to 10 servings

3 bananas, sliced
Lemon juice
4 oranges, peeled and cut into bite-sized pieces
1 cup chopped walnuts
1 cup shredded coconut
½ cup pitted fresh cherries, halved
¼ cup sugar
1 cup miniature marshmallows

Sprinkle banana slices with lemon juice to prevent browning. Combine all ingredients and toss gently.

Frozen Fantasy

Makes 8 servings

2 **3-ounce packages cream cheese, softened**
1 **cup mayonnaise**
3½ **cups canned fruit cocktail, drained**
½ **cup maraschino cherries**
2½ **cups miniature marshmallows**
1 **cup whipping cream**

Blend cream cheese with mayonnaise. Stir in fruit cocktail, cherries, and marshmallows. Fold in whipped cream and pour into a 2-quart casserole or two 1-quart round ice cream containers. Freeze until firm. To serve, let stand at room temperature for 10 minutes.

Melon Madness

Makes 8 servings

1 **cantaloupe**
1 **honeydew melon**
⅓ **watermelon**
4 **bananas**
4 **quarts strawberries**
4 **oranges, peeled and sectioned**
2 **cups pineapple juice**

Form melon balls with cantaloupe, honeydew, and watermelon. Slice bananas, halve strawberries, and cut oranges into bite-sized pieces. Combine all fruits and mix well with pineapple juice.

Fruit and Cheese Salad

Makes 4 to 6 servings

2 **3-ounce packages cream cheese, softened**
¼ **cup chopped green onions**
2 **tablespoons chopped parsley**
1 **cup plain yogurt**
2 **tablespoons orange marmalade**
½ **teaspoon vanilla extract**
4 **cups assorted fruits, cut into bite-sized pieces**
1 **cup croutons**
   Crisp lettuce leaves

In a small bowl blend first three ingredients. Shape into 20 balls (about ¾-inch in diameter); cover and chill. Blend yogurt, marmalade, and vanilla. Pour over fruit. Cover and chill. To serve, add cheese balls and croutons to fruit. Toss to blend. Spoon onto lettuce leaves.

Tropical Waldorf Salad _____

Makes 6 servings

2 firm, large bananas, peeled
  and sliced
2 large, tart apples, cored and
  sliced
1 cup diced celery
½ cup chopped dates
½ cup chopped walnuts
½ cup mayonnaise
2 tablespoons sour cream
1 teaspoon lemon juice
⅛ teaspoon ground ginger
  Crisp salad greens
¼ cup flaked coconut

Combine bananas, apples, celery, dates, and walnuts. For dressing, blend together mayonnaise, sour cream, lemon juice, and ginger. Pour over fruit and toss. Serve on crisp salad greens. Sprinkle with coconut.

Pineapple-Pecan Salad _____

Makes 4 servings

1 medium-sized pineapple
1 orange, cut into bite-sized
  pieces
1 kiwi, peeled and sliced
1 apple, cored and chopped
½ cup pecan halves
2 tablespoons fresh lime juice
1 tablespoon honey
1 tablespoon poppy seeds
1 teaspoon grated lime peel

Cut pineapple in half lengthwise through crown. Remove fruit from shell with a curved knife, leaving shell intact. Core and cut fruit into chunks. Measure out four cups pineapple and refrigerate remainder for later use. Combine 3 cups pineapple with orange, kiwi, apple, and pecans in large bowl. Place 1 cup pineapple and remaining ingredients in blender. Blend until smooth. Spoon fruit into pineapple shells if desired. Pour dressing over fruit and serve.

Honey-Lime Pineapple Salad _____

Makes 8 servings

1 fresh pineapple
3 large carrots, thinly sliced
1 honeydew melon, cut into chunks
½ cup slivered dates
¼ cup honey
2 tablespoons white wine vinegar
1 tablespoon vegetable oil
2 tablespoons lime juice
2 teaspoons grated lime peel

Twist crown from pineapple. Cut pineapple in half lengthwise, then in quarters. Remove fruit from shell; core and slice. Combine pineapple, carrots, melon, and dates in salad bowl. For dressing, whisk together remaining ingredients. Toss salad with dressing and serve.

Old-Fashioned Waldorf Salad _____

Makes 8 to 10 servings

4 medium apples
1 tablespoon lemon juice
½ cup chopped celery
½ cup halved seedless green grapes
½ cup chopped walnuts
¼ cup raisins
1 cup mayonnaise *or* salad dressing
1 tablespoon sugar
½ teaspoon lemon juice
Ground nutmeg

Core and dice apples (to make about 4 cups). In a large bowl sprinkle apples with 1 tablespoon lemon juice. Add celery, grapes, walnuts, and raisins. In a small bowl combine mayonnaise, sugar, and lemon juice. Mix well. Spoon dressing over the apple mixture. Sprinkle lightly with nutmeg. Cover and chill. To serve, fold dressing into fruit mixture.

Nutty Fruit Slaw

Makes 8 to 10 servings

1 8¼-ounce can sliced pineapple
1 tablespoon lemon juice
1 medium banana, sliced
3 cups finely shredded cabbage
1 cup thinly sliced celery
1 11-ounce can mandarin oranges, drained
½ cup chopped walnuts
¼ cup raisins
1 8-ounce carton orange yogurt
½ teaspoon salt

Drain pineapple, reserving 2 tablespoons of syrup. Cut into bite-sized pieces and set aside. Combine reserved syrup with lemon juice; then toss 1 tablespoon of mixture with banana slices. In serving bowl combine pineapple, banana, cabbage, celery, oranges, nuts, and raisins. Mix remaining juice mixture with yogurt and salt, then toss with cabbage mixture. Cover and chill before serving.

Guacamole Salad

Makes 2 servings

3 medium-sized avocados, peeled and seeded
1 thick slice of onion
2 tablespoons lemon juice
1 large clove garlic, minced
½ teaspoon salt
4 cups shredded lettuce
2 tomatoes, cut into eighths

Combine avocados, onion, lemon juice, garlic, and salt in a blender. Blend until smooth. Arrange lettuce on two plates and top with guacamole. Place tomato wedges around salad and serve.

Cheese-Stuffed Pears

Makes 6 servings

1 3-ounce package cream cheese, softened
2 tablespoons powdered sugar
1 tablespoon frozen orange juice concentrate
½ cup chopped pecans
6 whole pears, cored
6 sprigs fresh mint (optional)

In small bowl beat cheese and sugar until fluffy. Beat in orange juice concentrate. Mix in pecans. Spoon mixture into each pear. Serve with sprig of mint, if desired.

Overnight Fruit Salad

Makes 10 to 12 servings

1 20-ounce can pineapple chunks
3 slightly beaten egg yolks
1 tablespoon sugar
2 tablespoons vinegar
1 tablespoon butter *or* margarine
   Dash salt
1 16-ounce can pitted, light sweet cherries, drained
3 oranges, peeled and sectioned
2 cups miniature marshmallows
1 cup whipping cream

Reserving 2 tablespoons of syrup, drain pineapple. To prepare custard, in a small heavy saucepan combine pineapple syrup, egg yolks, sugar, vinegar, butter, and salt. Cook over low heat 6 minutes, stirring constantly until slightly thickened. Cool to room temperature. In serving bowl combine pineapple chunks, cherries, oranges, and marshmallows. Gently mix in custard. Beat whipping cream until soft peaks form and fold into custard and fruit mixture. Refrigerate overnight.

Seafood Specials

Herring and Beets

Makes 12 servings

2 cups minced cooked beets
1½ cups finely chopped herring in brine or wine sauce, drained
1 large potato, pared, cooked, and diced
¾ cup pared, cored, chopped apple
¼ cup chopped onion
1 cup sour cream
2 teaspoons dried dillweed
1 teaspoon prepared mustard

Combine beets, herring, potato, apple, and onion in medium bowl. Mix sour cream, dill, and mustard; stir into salad. Refrigerate, covered, until chilled (about 2 hours).

Tuna Tater Salad

Makes 4 servings

1 9¼-ounce can tuna, drained
2 stalks celery, chopped
2 carrots, shredded
½ small onion, chopped
8 pitted ripe olives, sliced
¾ cup mayonnaise *or* salad dressing
1 teaspoon lemon juice
1 teaspoon prepared mustard
1½ cups shoestring potatoes, cooked
Lettuce leaves

Flake tuna with a fork. In medium bowl combine tuna, celery, carrots, onion, and olives; set aside. To make dressing, combine mayonnaise, lemon juice, and mustard. Add to tuna mixture and toss. Cover and chill. Just before serving mix in shoestring potatoes. Serve on bed of lettuce.

Spicy Salad Baskets

Makes 4 servings

- 8 **large prawns, cooked and cleaned**
- 1 **cup hot chili salsa**
  Juice of one lemon
- 4 **10-inch flour tortillas**
  Oil
- 1 **ripe avocado**
- ⅓ **cup mayonnaise**
- ¼ **cup sour cream**
- 2 **tablespoons lemon juice**
- 2 **tablespoons hot chili salsa**
- ⅛ **teaspoon salt**
  Pepper to taste
- 1 **fresh pineapple**
- 1 **cantaloupe** *or* **papaya, peeled and sliced**
- 1 **tomato, quartered**

Marinate prawns in salsa and lemon juice overnight in refrigerator. Preheat oven to 400°. Oil both sides of each tortilla. Press each tortilla into a 1½-pint round baking dish and arrange edges to ruffle. Hold shape by packing foil into bottom of each tortilla. Bake for 7 minutes. Remove foil and bake until golden (1 minute); cool. For dressing, mash avocado and mix with mayonnaise, sour cream, lemon juice, salsa, salt, and pepper. Set aside. Twist crown from pineapple. Cut pineapple in half lengthwise, then in quarters. Remove fruit from shell; core and slice. Arrange prawns, pineapple, cantaloupe, and tomato in tortilla baskets. Garnish with pineapple slices and serve with avocado dressing.

Crunchy Salmon Salad Spread

Makes 5 servings

- 1 **1-pound can salmon, drained and flaked**
- 1 **8-ounce can water chestnuts, drained and chopped**
- 1 **small onion, minced**
- 1 **stalk celery, minced**
- ½ **cup mayonnaise**
- 2 **tablespoons soy sauce**
- 1 **tablespoon lemon juice**

Combine all ingredients and mix well. Serve on bread or crackers. Garnish with parsley, if desired.

Curried Shrimp Salad

Makes 4 to 6 servings

3 **cups cooked rice**
1 **pound shrimp, cooked, shelled, and deveined**
½ **cup sliced celery**
½ **cup sliced green onion**
½ **cup julienne-cut green pepper**
⅓ **cup julienne-cut red pepper**
⅔ **cup bottled herb and garlic dressing**
1 **teaspoon curry powder**
1 **cup croutons**
  Crisp lettuce leaves

In a large bowl combine first 8 ingredients. Toss to mix. Cover and refrigerate several hours to blend flavors. To serve, toss in croutons. Spoon onto lettuce leaves.

Crabmeat Salad

Makes 8 servings

4 **cups cooked crabmeat**
½ **teaspoon salt**
⅛ **teaspoon paprika**
  French dressing (enough to cover)
  Lettuce
1 **cup mayonnaise**
1 **2-ounce jar pimiento**
1 **cup cubed cucumber**

Check crabmeat for shells, then mix with salt and paprika. Cover with French dressing and marinate in refrigerator until completely chilled. Line salad bowl with a bed of lettuce and arrange crabmeat in bottom. Spread with mayonnaise and top with strips of pimiento and cucumber.

Fruit and Cheese Salad, 5
Curried Shrimp Salad, this page

Salade Nicoise

Makes 4 servings

Boston lettuce leaves
2 7½-ounce cans of water-packed tuna, drained
1 2-ounce can flat anchovies
2 cups diced new potatoes, boiled
2 tablespoons chopped parsley
¼ cup drained capers
2 cups whole green beans, cooked
2 shallots, peeled and minced
½ cup pitted black olives
1 2-ounce jar whole pimiento, drained
4 hard-boiled eggs, peeled and halved
2 large tomatoes, cut into eighths
1 cup seasoned croutons French or vinaigrette dressing

Arrange bed of lettuce on a serving platter. Break tuna into large chunks and place in one area of platter; top with anchovy fillets. Toss potatoes with parsley and capers; arrange next to tuna. Toss beans with shallots and place next to potato mixture. Also arrange olives, pimiento, eggs, tomatoes, and croutons in separate areas on lettuce. Just before serving pour dressing over salad.

Tuna Salad

Makes 2 servings

1 8-ounce package cream cheese
1 13-ounce can tuna, drained
1 tablespoon dry sherry
1 tablespoon lemon juice
½ teaspoon garlic powder
½ teaspoon dillweed
⅛ teaspoon white pepper
2 medium-sized tomatoes
Black olives

Combine all ingredients except tomatoes and olives. Mix until light and fluffy. Cut off tops of tomatoes in a zigzag pattern. Scoop out seeds and discard. Fill tomatoes with tuna salad and garnish with black olives, if desired.

South Sea Salad

Makes 4 servings

1 **cantaloupe, peeled, sliced into 4 rings**
   Lettuce leaves
1 **pound cooked shrimp, cleaned**
2 **firm bananas, sliced**
1 **pound red grape clusters**
1 **ripe banana**
1 **cup mayonnaise**
¼ **cup chutney**
2 **tablespoons lemon juice**

Arrange each cantaloupe ring on lettuce-lined salad plate. Fill centers with shrimp and surround with banana, oranges, and grape clusters. For dressing, mash banana with a fork. Combine with mayonnaise, chutney, and lemon juice; mix until thoroughly blended and pour over each salad.

Shrimp and Scallop Salad

Makes 4 servings

Seafood Salad Dressing (p.62)
1 **pound small shrimp, cleaned**
1 **pound bay scallops**
1 **6-ounce package frozen crabmeat, thawed and flaked**
1 **cup frozen green peas, thawed**
¼ **cup sliced green onion** *or* **scallions**
3 **cups shredded fresh spinach leaves**

Prepare dressing and chill. Boil 4 quarts of salted water. Drop shrimp in and cook 1 to 2 minutes or until almost tender. Add scallops and cook until just tender and cooked through. Drain and cool to room temperature. Toss shrimp and scallops with crabmeat, peas, onion, and dressing. Arrange spinach on platter and top with seafood salad.

Pasta Pleasers

Shell Salad

Makes 4 servings

2½ cups (8 ounces) uncooked small shell pasta
2 cups diced cooked chicken
½ cup diced celery
½ cup finely chopped carrot
½ cup sweet pickle relish
½ cup mayonnaise
2 tablespoons chopped onion
Salt and pepper

Cook shells according to package directions. Rinse under cold water and drain. Combine remaining ingredients in large bowl; mix well. Add shells and toss to coat. Chill before serving.

Italian Macaroni Salad

Makes 4 servings

1¾ cups uncooked rotini noodles
¼ pound thinly sliced pepperoni
1 cup thinly sliced zucchini
1 cup coarsely chopped green pepper
½ cup halved black olives
¼ cup chopped fresh parsley
¼ cup chopped pimiento
2 tablespoons sliced green onion
¾ cup olive oil
3 tablespoons wine vinegar
1 clove garlic, minced
1 tablespoon Dijon-style mustard
½ teaspoon salt
¼ teaspoon pepper

Cook noodles according to package directions; rinse under cold water and drain. Combine noodles, pepperoni, zucchini, green pepper, olives, parsley, pimiento, and green onion in a large bowl; toss gently. In small bowl combine oil, vinegar, garlic, mustard, salt, and pepper. Whip with a whisk until thick and creamy. Pour ½ of dressing over salad and serve the rest on the side.

Macaroni Chicken Salad _____

Makes 6 servings

1 7-ounce package ring
   macaroni
1 cup cubed cooked chicken
1 cup diced celery
2 teaspoons chopped parsley
1¼ cups mayonnaise
1 tablespoon sugar
1 cup diced apple
½ cup chopped nuts
1 teaspoon salt
½ cup pickle relish
   Lettuce leaves
3 hard-boiled eggs, halved
   Green olives

Cook macaroni according to package directions until tender. Rinse under cold water and drain. In a large bowl mix all ingredients except lettuce, eggs, and olives. Place salad on bed of lettuce and garnish with eggs and olives.

Pasta Primavera _____

Makes 4 servings

½ pound spaghetti, cooked and
   drained
1 8-ounce bottle herb and garlic
   or Italian dressing
½ teaspoon minced garlic
3 cups diced cooked chicken
¼ cup mayonnaise
1 pint cherry tomatoes, halved
1 cup sliced green onions *or*
   scallions
¼ pound fresh mushrooms,
   sliced
1 large green pepper, thinly
   sliced
1½ cups croutons

Toss hot pasta with ¾ cup salad dressing and garlic. Reserve remaining dressing. Cover and chill for at least 2 hours. Just before serving toss chicken with mayonnaise and then with pasta. Arrange on a serving dish and top with remaining ingredients.

Nectarine Pork Pasta

Makes 8 servings

½ **cup vegetable oil**
½ **cup white wine vinegar**
3 **tablespoons minced chives**
1½ **teaspoons salt**
1½ **teaspoons dry mustard**
1 **teaspoon crushed leaf
  summer savory**
½ **teaspoon black pepper**
3 **cups julienne-cut cooked
  pork**
3 **cups cooked rotelle, shell, *or*
  elbow macaroni**
1 **pound nectarines, peeled
  and sliced (about 4)**
1 **small cucumber, sliced
  Lettuce leaves**

With a wire whisk blend oil, vinegar, chives, salt, mustard, savory, and pepper in a large bowl. Add pork, pasta, nectarines, and cucumber; toss gently and chill for several hours to blend flavors. Serve on a bed of lettuce.

Ziti Tomato Mix

Makes 8 servings

1 **pound uncooked ziti**
2 **medium tomatoes, chopped**
1 **cup chopped sweet pickle**
1 **cup chopped green pepper**
½ **cup chopped onion**
½ **cup chopped celery**
1¾ **cups mayonnaise *or* salad
  dressing**
¾ **cup sour cream**
1 **teaspoon spicy brown
  mustard**
½ **teaspoon salt**
⅛ **teaspoon ground white
  pepper
  Lettuce leaves**
1 **small tomato, sliced
  Minced parsley**

Cook ziti according to directions until al dente (tender but firm to bite). Drain and cool to room temperature. Mix in tomato, pickle, green pepper, onion, and celery. Mix mayonnaise, sour cream, mustard, salt, and pepper; stir into ziti mixture. Chill for 3 or 4 hours to blend flavors, then serve on bed of lettuce. Garnish with sliced tomato and parsley.

Cool Vegetable Pasta Salad

Makes 6 servings

½ pound uncooked thin
   spaghetti
1 small zucchini, sliced
1 7-ounce can artichoke hearts,
   drained and halved
4 ounces fresh asparagus
1 large carrot, sliced
½ cup chopped onion
1 clove garlic, minced
2 tablespoons butter *or*
   margarine
2 tablespoons olive *or*
   vegetable oil
½ teaspoon dried basil
¼ teaspoon dried oregano
½ teaspoon salt
   Dash pepper
   Freshly grated nutmeg
¼ cup grated Parmesan cheese
   Red *or* green pepper rings

Cook spaghetti according to directions until al dente (almost tender); cool. Sauté vegetables in butter and oil in large skillet until still crisp but tender. Sprinkle with herbs, salt, and pepper. Cool. Toss vegetables with spaghetti; place on serving dish. Sprinkle with nutmeg and cheese. Garnish with pepper rings.

Fruity Macaroni

Makes 6 servings

1 8-ounce package elbow
   macaroni
½ cup wheat germ
1 13-ounce can pineapple
   tidbits
1 cup cantaloupe balls
1 cup seedless grapes, halved
1 8-ounce carton mandarin
   orange yogurt
2 tablespoons honey

Cook macaroni according to package directions. Rinse under cold water and drain. Reserve 2 tablespoons wheat germ and add remaining wheat germ to macaroni. Reserve pineapple juice and add tidbits to macaroni. Also add cantaloupe and grapes. Toss. Combine yogurt, honey, and 2 tablespoons pineapple juice. Mix well and pour over macaroni mixture. Garnish with wheat germ and chill before serving.

Main Dish Salads

Chicken Salad Spread

Makes 2 servings

2 cups diced cooked chicken
¼ cup celery, finely chopped
½ cup mayonnaise
2 tablespoons sour cream
1 tablespoon sherry
1 tablespoon lemon juice
½ cup ripe olives, halved
Paprika

Mix together chicken, celery, mayonnaise, sour cream, and sherry. Garnish with olives and sprinkle with paprika. Serve with crackers.

Ham Salad Spread

Makes 2 servings

1 cup chopped cooked ham
¼ cup finely grated Cheddar cheese
1 teaspoon prepared mustard
2 teaspoons pickle relish
3 tablespoons mayonnaise

Combine all ingredients and mix well. Serve on crackers or bread.

Beef and Walnut Salad Spread

Makes 1 serving

1 ounce roast beef, finely chopped
1 sweet pickle, finely chopped
2 tablespoons chopped walnuts
1 teaspoon diced onion
½ teaspoon prepared mustard
2 to 3 tablespoons mayonnaise *or* salad dressing

Mix all ingredients. Serve on rye bread or with crackers.

Layered Chef's Salad

Makes 4 servings

Herbed Yogurt Dressing (p. 59)
- 4 **cups torn lettuce**
- 4 **scallions, sliced**
- 3 **large tomatoes, cut in wedges**
- ½ **cup chopped fresh basil**
- ½ **pound regular *or* smoked mozzarella cheese, shredded**
- 1 **cup alfalfa sprouts**
- 1 **red onion, sliced**
- 4 **ounces hard salami, julienne-cut**
- 2 **hard-boiled eggs, chopped**
- ½ **pound smoked turkey breast, julienne-cut**
- 1 **red pepper, cut in rings**
- 1 **cup watercress leaves**
- 1 **cup croutons**

Make dressing and chill. In a large glass bowl layer lettuce with scallions, tomatoes, basil, cheese, alfalfa sprouts, onion, salami, eggs, turkey, pepper, watercress, and croutons. Cover and chill until serving time. To serve, scoop salad onto individual plates and top with dressing.

Mexican Salad

Makes 6 servings

- 4 **cups shredded lettuce**
- 4 **cups tortilla chips**
- 1½ **cups canned refried beans**
- 1 **cup taco sauce**
- 2 **cups coarsely shredded Cheddar cheese**
- ½ **cup black olives, sliced**
- 2 **tomatoes, diced**
- 2 **tablespoons minced green onion**
  Sour cream
  Diced green chili peppers

Place lettuce in center of large serving platter. Surround with tortilla chips. Top with refried beans, taco sauce, and cheese. Broil 1 minute or until cheese melts. Add remaining toppings and serve with sour cream and chili peppers.

Hot German Potato Salad _____

Makes 8 servings

7 **medium potatoes**
6 **slices bacon**
½ **cup sugar**
3 **tablespoons flour**
2 **teaspoons seasoned salt**
1 **teaspoon caraway seed**
½ **teaspoon ground mustard**
¼ **teaspoon ground black**
   pepper
1 **cup water**
1 **cup cider vinegar**
1 **tablespoon chives**

Boil potatoes until tender; slice when cool. In large skillet cook bacon pieces; let drain on a paper towel and crumble. Combine sugar, flour, seasoned salt, caraway seed, mustard, and pepper; blend into bacon drippings. Cook over medium heat to make smooth paste (one to two minutes). Blend in water and vinegar. Bring to a boil, stirring constantly. Boil two to three minutes then remove from heat. Gently stir in potatoes and chives. Let stand three or four hours to blend flavors. Heat in 350° oven for 10 minutes before serving. Garnish with bacon and chives, if desired.

Stuffed Pepper Salad _____

Makes 4 servings

2 **cups shredded cabbage**
1 **cup diced cooked ham**
   or **cooked beef**
½ **cup shredded carrot**
¼ **cup sliced radish**
¼ **cup chopped cucumber**
1 **8-ounce carton plain yogurt**
2 **teaspoons sugar**
1 **teaspoon lemon juice**
½ **teaspoon celery seed**
¼ **teaspoon garlic salt**
¼ **teaspoon onion salt**
   Dash pepper
2 **large bell peppers**

In a medium-sized bowl combine cabbage, ham, carrot, radish, and cucumber. Blend yogurt, sugar, lemon juice, celery seed, garlic salt, onion salt, and pepper. Pour over vegetable mixture; toss to coat. Chill for one hour. Remove tops from peppers and cut lengthwise. Remove seeds. Spoon vegetable mixture into peppers and serve.

Reuben Salad

Makes 4 servings

5   slices rye bread
3   tablespoons butter *or* margarine
8   cups torn lettuce
1   cup chilled cooked corned beef *or* 2 3-ounce packages sliced corned beef, cut into thin strips
1   8-ounce can sauerkraut, chilled, drained, and snipped
1   cup (4 ounces) cubed Swiss cheese
¾   cup Thousand Island dressing
½   teaspoon caraway seed

Brush both sides of rye bread slices with butter. Cut into ½-inch cubes and spread on a cookie sheet. Bake at 300° for 20 to 25 minutes. Cubes should be crisp. Makes two cups. Store half of croutons in a covered container in refrigerator. Mix lettuce, corned beef, sauerkraut, cheese, and 1 cup croutons in bowl. Combine dressing and caraway seeds and pour over salad.

Spring Spinach Salad

Makes 4 servings

1   pound fresh spinach
⅓   cup sliced green onions *or* scallions
5   slices bacon, cut in thirds
2   tablespoons red wine vinegar
1   tablespoon lemon juice
1   teaspoon sugar
½   teaspoon salt
⅛   teaspoon ground pepper
2   hard-boiled eggs, peeled and chopped
1½ cups croutons

Wash spinach and tear into bite-sized pieces. Mix with green onions and chill until serving time. Just before serving fry bacon in a large skillet until crisp. Add vinegar, lemon juice, sugar, salt, and pepper; cook until sugar dissolves. Add spinach mixture to skillet and cook, tossing continually until spinach is slightly wilted. Remove to serving bowl. Add chopped eggs and croutons; toss and serve immediately.

Kona Ham Hawaiian

Makes 4 servings

1 20-ounce can pineapple chunks, 1 tablespoon juice reserved
½ pound cooked ham, cut into strips
½ cup sliced celery
1 banana, sliced
1 cup halved strawberries
½ cup mayonnaise
¼ teaspoon dried mustard
Lettuce

Combine pineapple, ham, celery, banana, and strawberries in a bowl. Combine mayonnaise, mustard, and reserved pineapple juice; toss with salad. Serve on bed of lettuce.

Five Bean Salad

Makes 10 to 12 servings

8 slices bacon
⅔ cup sugar
2 tablespoons cornstarch
1½ teaspoons salt
Dash pepper
¾ cup vinegar
½ cup water
1 16-ounce can cut green beans, drained
1 16-ounce can lima beans, drained
1 16-ounce can cut wax beans, drained
1 15½-ounce can red kidney beans, drained
1 15-ounce can garbanzo beans, drained

In large skillet cook bacon until crisp, reserving ¼ cup drippings in skillet. Remove bacon and crumble; set aside. Combine sugar, cornstarch, salt, and pepper and stir into drippings. Add vinegar and water; cook and stir until boiling. Stir beans into skillet. Cover and simmer for 15 to 20 minutes. Stir in bacon and place on serving dish.

East-West Pork Salad

Makes 4 servings

1 **pound boneless pork loin, cut into thin strips**
Salt and pepper
½ **teaspoon ground coriander**
¼ **teaspoon red pepper flakes**
¼ **teaspoon ground ginger**
1 **tablespoon vegetable oil**
1 **clove garlic, pressed**
1 **20-ounce can pineapple tidbits, juice reserved**
2 **tablespoons sweetened coconut juice *or* coconut cream**
1 **tablespoon peanut butter**
½ **cup sliced celery**
¼ **cup sliced green onion**
1 **cup chow mein noodles**
Lettuce leaves

Sprinkle pork with salt and pepper, coriander, pepper flakes, and ginger. Brown in oil with garlic. Add reserved pineapple juice; cover; simmer 10 minutes. Remove pork from skillet. Stir in coconut juice and peanut butter. Simmer 3 to 5 minutes until slightly thickened. Cool. Mix pork with pineapple, celery, and onion. Mix with cooled sauce. Toss with noodles and serve on a bed of lettuce.

Shanghai Salad

Makes 4 servings

1 **bunch fresh spinach**
2 **bananas, sliced**
1 **honeydew melon, peeled and sliced**
1 **orange, peeled and sliced**
1 **pound diced cooked chicken *or* turkey**
¼ **pound bean sprouts**
1 **ripe banana**
1 **cup mayonnaise**
1 **tablespoon soy sauce**
1 **teaspoon curry powder**
Pinch garlic powder
Grape clusters

Line four salad plates with spinach leaves. Arrange bananas, melon, orange, chicken, and sprouts on spinach. For dressing, mash banana with a fork and blend with mayonnaise, soy sauce, curry powder, and garlic powder. Pour over salads and serve with garnish of grape clusters.

Tarragon Chicken Salad _____

Makes 4 servings

Creamy Tarragon Dressing (p. 61)
4 small avocados
   Lettuce leaves
2 cups diced cooked chicken
2 firm bananas, sliced
1 orange, peeled and sectioned
1 green bell pepper, diced

Prepare dressing and chill. Peel avocados and cut in half. Remove seed and place one avocado half on each of four plates lined with lettuce leaves. In a bowl combine chicken, bananas, orange, and bell pepper; toss. Fill each avocado half with chicken salad. Garnish with extra fruit, if desired. Serve with dressing.

Oriental Chicken Salad _____

Makes 2 servings

1 8-ounce can chunk pineapple
3 tablespoons vegetable oil
2 tablespoons soy sauce
2 tablespoons white wine vinegar
2 tablespoons toasted sesame seeds
1 tablespoon Dijon-style mustard
¼ teaspoon Chinese five spices
1 quart shredded lettuce
½ cup cilantro *or* parsley
¼ cup chopped green onion
2 cups diced cooked chicken
½ red bell pepper, sliced
½ cup sliced water chestnuts
   Chow mein noodles

Drain pineapple, reserving 2 tablespoons juice. Combine juice with oil, soy sauce, vinegar, sesame seeds, mustard, and spices. Spoon half of dressing over chicken. Toss lettuce, cilantro, and green onion; divide onto two salad plates. Arrange chicken, pineapple, pepper, and water chestnuts on lettuce. Serve with noodles and remainder of dressing.

Tempting Tosses

Watercress Toss

Makes 4 servings

2 to 3 bunches watercress,
    leaves only
16 cherry tomatoes
3 tablespoons olive oil
1 tablespoon lemon juice
½ teaspoon prepared mustard
1 clove garlic, minced
    Salt and pepper to taste

Carefully wash and dry watercress and tomatoes. Arrange in a bowl. Combine remaining ingredients and mix well. Pour over salad and toss to coat.

Caesar Salad

Makes 6 servings

2 tablespoons anchovy paste
1 clove garlic, minced
¼ teaspoon salt
    Dash pepper
2 whole eggs
7 tablespoons olive oil
4 tablespoons wine vinegar
2 tablespoons lemon juice
1 large head lettuce, washed
    and dried
1½ cups seasoned croutons
½ cup Parmesan cheese

In small bowl combine anchovy paste, garlic, salt, pepper, and eggs. Mix well. Stir in oil, vinegar, and lemon juice. In large bowl add dressing to lettuce leaves and toss. Add croutons and toss again. Garnish with Parmesan cheese.

Spinach-Cabbage Salad _____

Makes 4 servings

1½ **cups coarsely chopped**
    spinach leaves
2 **cups shredded red cabbage**
⅓ **teaspoon salt**
¼ **teaspoon celery seed**
3 **tablespoons chopped olives**
    or **chives**
1 **cup cottage cheese**
    Lettuce leaves
    Mayonnaise

Toss together spinach, cabbage, salt, celery seed, olives, and cottage cheese. Serve on a bed of lettuce with mayonnaise.

Cracked Wheat Salad _____

Makes 6 servings

1 **cup bulgur (cracked) wheat**
2 **cups boiling water**
    Salt
½ **cup chopped green onion**
½ **cup diced carrot**
½ **cup diced celery**
2 **tomatoes, sliced**
½ **cup alfalfa sprouts**
⅔ **cup minced parsley**
    Black pepper
6 **tablespoons olive oil**
2 **teaspoons wine vinegar**
    Salt

Pour boiling water over wheat in a small bowl. Cover and let stand for 30 minutes. Drain and place in large serving bowl. Let cool completely and salt to taste. Combine carrot, celery, tomatoes, sprouts, parsley, and pepper; add to wheat. Combine remaining ingredients and pour over salad. Serve cold.

South-of-the-Border Salad

Makes 6 servings

4 cups shredded iceberg lettuce
4 cups shredded romaine lettuce
4 medium-sized beets, fresh-cooked *or* canned, thinly sliced
4 oranges, peeled and sliced
3 bananas, sliced
2 grapefruit, peeled and sliced
2 unpeeled red apples, cut in wedges
2 unpeeled green apples, cut in wedges
3 limes, peeled and sliced
  Seed of 2 pomegranates
½ cup unsalted peanuts
  Poppy Seed Dressing (p. 62)

Place lettuce and romaine in large glass serving bowl. Arrange beets and fruit over lettuce. Sprinkle with seeds and nuts. Prepare dressing and pour over salad.

Mushroom Salad

Makes 8 servings

1½ pounds fresh mushrooms
½ cup vegetable oil
¼ cup red wine vinegar
1 tablespoon lemon juice
1 teaspoon sugar
1 tablespoon snipped fresh chives
⅛ teaspoon garlic powder
¾ teaspoon salt
½ teaspoon pepper

Wash mushrooms and slice. Place in serving bowl. Combine remaining ingredients and mix well. Pour over mushrooms and toss.

Tomato-Pepper Shake

Makes 4 servings

⅓ **cup olive oil**
¼ **cup white wine vinegar**
2 **teaspoons sugar**
1 **teaspoon snipped chives**
½ **teaspoon dry mustard**
½ **teaspoon crushed dried basil**
3 **cups torn romaine**
3 **large tomatoes, cut into bite-sized pieces**
1 **small green pepper, coarsely chopped**

Combine oil, vinegar, sugar, chives, mustard, and basil; mix well. In a salad bowl toss romaine, tomatoes, and green pepper. Mix dressing again and pour over salad.

California Salad

Makes 6 servings

2 **cups shredded zucchini**
1 **cup shredded carrots**
1 **cup alfalfa** *or* **bean sprouts**
½ **cup honey**
⅓ **cup vegetable oil**
⅓ **cup distilled white vinegar**

In a medium-sized bowl combine zucchini, carrots, and bean sprouts. Combine remaining ingredients and mix well. Pour over vegetables and toss.

Green and White Asparagus Salad

Makes 8 servings

Creamy Tarragon Dressing (p. 61)
1 **pound fresh asparagus**
2 **16-ounce cans white asparagus, drained and chilled**
Lettuce
1 **small cucumber, sliced**
Pimiento strips

Prepare dressing and chill. Cook fresh asparagus in boiling water until crisp-tender (2 to 3 minutes). Drain; rinse under cold water and drain again. Chill for several minutes. Cut all asparagus into bite-sized pieces and place on bed of lettuce. Pour dressing over salad and toss to coat. Garnish with cucumber and pimiento.

Sunny Salsa Salad

Makes 6 servings

1 fresh pineapple
1 head iceberg lettuce, torn
1 head romaine lettuce, torn
2 tomatoes, chopped
1 15¼-ounce can kidney beans, drained
1 7¾-ounce can whole pitted ripe olives, drained
1 cup sour cream
½ cup hot chili salsa
½ pound shredded Cheddar cheese

Twist crown from pineapple. Cut pineapple in half lengthwise, then in quarters. Remove fruit from shell. Trim off core and cut into chunks. Place lettuce in large salad bowl. Add pineapple, tomatoes, kidney beans, and olives. For dressing, in small bowl mix sour cream and salsa. Toss salad with dressing. Top each serving with cheese.

Pineapple-Spinach Salad

Makes 4 servings

1 fresh pineapple
1 bunch spinach leaves
4 bacon strips, cooked and crumbled
4 hard-boiled eggs, chopped
1 red onion, sliced
6 tablespoons vegetable oil
2 tablespoons white wine vinegar
1 teaspoon crumbled sweet basil
½ teaspoon dry mustard

Twist crown from pineapple. Cut pineapple in half lengthwise, then in quarters. Remove fruit from shell; core and slice. Add spinach, bacon, eggs, onion, and pineapple to salad bowl. For dressing, whisk together remaining ingredients. Toss salad with dressing and serve immediately on chilled plates.

Mexican Salad, 25;
Sunny Salsa Salad, this page;
Corn Relish, 46

Cucumber Salad

Makes 4 servings

2 cucumbers, peeled and
sliced
1 green pepper, diced
1 tomato, cut in eighths
1 small onion, sliced
¼ cup sugar
½ cup vinegar
1 cup water
¼ cup vegetable oil
Salt and pepper to taste

Combine cucumbers, pepper, tomato, and onion in serving bowl. Mix sugar, vinegar, water, and oil. Pour over vegetables and season with salt and pepper; toss.

Vinaigrette Coleslaw

Makes 8 servings

1 8-ounce can crushed pineapple, ⅓ cup juice reserved
7 cups finely shredded
cabbage
1 cup shredded carrots
½ cup chopped green pepper
¼ cup minced onion
¼ cup vegetable oil
¼ cup sandwich and salad
sauce
3 tablespoons white wine
vinegar
1 tablespoon sugar
⅛ teaspoon dry mustard
Dash ground allspice
⅛ teaspoon ground white
pepper

Mix pineapple, cabbage, carrots, green pepper, and onion in salad bowl. Shake reserved pineapple juice and remaining ingredients in screw-top jar; pour over cabbage mixture and toss. Refrigerate until serving time.

Hearts of Palm Salad _____

Makes 6 servings

1 head red leaf lettuce
3 tomatoes, sliced
1 onion, sliced
½ cup black olives, sliced
1 14-ounce can hearts of palm
2 tablespoons olive oil
4 tablespoons vegetable oil
4 tablespoons tarragon vinegar
¼ teaspoon crushed tarragon
½ teaspoon salt
¼ teaspoon freshly ground
   black pepper

Tear lettuce into bite-sized pieces. Gently toss together lettuce, tomatoes, onion, and olives. Drain hearts of palm and cut into bite-sized pieces; sprinkle over salad. Mix remaining ingredients well and pour over salad. Chill until serving time.

Avocado and Tomato Salad _____

Makes 6 servings

12 leaves lettuce
 1 tablespoon lime juice
 3 ripe avocados, pared and
   sliced
 2 tomatoes, sliced
 2 cloves garlic, peeled and
   minced
 ¼ cup vegetable oil
 ¼ cup tarragon vinegar
 ¼ teaspoon salt
   Dash pepper
 3 green onions, minced

Arrange 2 leaves of lettuce on each serving plate. Sprinkle lime juice over avocados. Arrange avocados and tomatoes in a fan on top of lettuce. Combine remaining ingredients; mix well and pour on salad. Garnish with green onion.

Orange-Almond Salad

Makes 6 servings

Creamy Tarragon Dressing (p. 61)
2 **medium heads romaine lettuce**
1 **11-ounce can mandarin oranges, drained**
4 **scallions, thinly sliced**
1 **tablespoon finely chopped fresh parsley**
½ **cup slivered almonds, toasted**

Make dressing and chill. Tear romaine into bite-sized pieces. Mix with oranges, scallions, parsley, and dressing. Sprinkle with almonds and serve.

Nutty Vegetable Salad

Makes 4 servings

4 **cups iceberg lettuce, torn into bite-sized pieces**
1 **small bunch watercress, leaves only**
1 **small red onion, thinly sliced**
3 **tablespoons lemon juice Salt and pepper**
1 **cup julienne-cut carrots**
1 **cup julienne-cut zucchini**
1 **cup julienne-cut Cheddar cheese**
½ **cup chopped walnuts**
1 **cup chopped peanuts Celery-Dill Dressing (p. 60)**

Combine lettuce, watercress, onion, and lemon juice in large serving bowl. Add salt and pepper to taste. Combine carrots, zucchini, and cheese; sprinkle over lettuce mixture. Top with walnuts and peanuts. Serve with Celery-Dill Dressing.

Zesty Marinades

Insalada Rosa

Makes 6 to 8 servings

3 cups cooked and sliced new potatoes
2 small zucchinis, sliced
1 cup chopped celery
2 medium tomatoes, cut in wedges
½ cup sliced stuffed olives
½ cup olive oil
3 tablespoons wine vinegar
¼ cup chopped parsley
½ teaspoon salt
¼ teaspoon oregano
⅛ teaspoon pepper
Lettuce leaves
1 cup croutons
3 tablespoons grated Parmesan cheese

In a bowl combine vegetables. Combine oil, vinegar, parsley, and seasonings; mix well. Pour over vegetables and toss. Cover and refrigerate for 2 hours. Serve on bed of lettuce and sprinkle with croutons and cheese.

Three Bean Salad

Makes 6 to 8 servings

1 8-ounce can cut wax beans
1 8-ounce can green beans
1 8-ounce can red kidney beans
1 medium onion, thinly sliced and separated into rings
½ cup chopped green pepper
⅔ cup vinegar
½ cup salad oil
¼ cup sugar
Salt and pepper to taste

Drain the canned beans. In a large bowl combine the wax beans, green beans, red kidney beans, onion rings, and green pepper. In a screw-top jar combine vinegar, salad oil, sugar, and salt and pepper; cover and shake well. Pour vinegar mixture over vegetables and stir lightly. Cover and chill at least 6 hours or overnight, stirring occasionally. Drain before serving.

Cauliflower Salad

Makes 8 servings

1 **medium head of cauliflower, broken into flowerets**
½ **cup French dressing**
1 **small avocado, diced**
½ **cup sliced stuffed green olives**
3 **tomatoes, cut into eighths**
½ **cup crumbled Roquefort cheese**
Crisp salad greens

Cover cauliflowerets with ice water; chill 1 hour. Drain. Add dressing and let stand 2 hours. Just before serving add avocado, olives, tomatoes, and cheese. Toss lightly. Serve on crisp greens.

Antipasto Salad

Makes 8 to 10 servings

⅔ **cup vinegar**
⅔ **cup vegetable oil**
4 **teaspoons instant chopped onion**
1 **teaspoon sugar**
1 **teaspoon garlic salt**
½ **teaspoon Italian seasoning**
½ **teaspoon basil, crumbled**
½ **teaspoon oregano, crumbled**
½ **teaspoon black pepper**
4 **cups (12 ounces) sliced mushrooms**
2 **carrots, sliced in rounds**
1 **14-ounce can artichoke hearts, drained and quartered**
1 **cup diagonally sliced celery**
1 **cup halved, pitted ripe olives**
½ **cup halved green olives**
1 **2-ounce jar sliced pimiento, drained**
Lettuce

Combine vinegar, oil, onion, sugar, and seasonings in saucepan. Bring to a boil; reduce heat and simmer, uncovered, 10 minutes. Combine remaining ingredients except lettuce in large bowl. Pour in hot marinade; stir and cover. Chill several hours or overnight, stirring occasionally. Serve in lettuce cups.

Carrot and Raisin Salad

Makes 6 servings

3 cups grated carrots
1 cup seedless raisins
1 tablespoon honey
6 tablespoons mayonnaise
¼ cup milk
1 tablespoon fresh lemon juice
¼ teaspoon salt

Combine carrots and raisins in serving bowl. Blend together remaining ingredients and pour over carrots and raisins. Stir thoroughly and chill to blend flavors.

Marinated Onion Salad

Makes 6 servings

½ cup olive oil
2 tablespoons lemon juice
½ teaspoon salt
¼ teaspoon ground pepper
½ teaspoon sugar
½ cup blue cheese, crumbled
4 large red onions, sliced

In a small bowl combine oil, lemon juice, salt, pepper, and sugar. Mix well. Stir in blue cheese. Place onion slices in dressing, making sure all are covered. Cover and refrigerate overnight.

Corn Relish

Makes 4 to 6 servings

2 cups cider vinegar
1⅓ cups sugar
1 teaspoon dried basil
¼ teaspoon pepper
1 cup chopped red bell pepper
½ cup chopped celery
2½ cups cooked corn, cut off the cob

Heat vinegar, sugar, basil, and pepper to boiling. Reduce heat and simmer 10 minutes. Stir in peppers and celery. Simmer 3 minutes. Stir in corn; simmer 5 minutes. Remove from heat and chill.

Deviled Egg Salad

Makes 8 servings

12 hard-boiled eggs, coarsely chopped
½ cup diced celery
¼ cup sliced green olives
¼ cup chopped sweet pickle
2 tablespoons minced onion
1 cup mayonnaise *or* salad dressing
½ teaspoon Worcestershire sauce
2 teaspoons spicy brown mustard
Paprika

Mix eggs, celery, olives, pickle, and onion in medium-sized bowl. Mix remaining ingredients except paprika; pour over egg mixture and toss. Refrigerate several hours for flavors to blend. Spoon into serving bowl; sprinkle with paprika.

Beet and Cucumber Salad

Makes 6 servings

1 16-ounce can sliced beets, drained
1 cucumber, peeled and sliced
½ cup vegetable oil
2 tablespoons white wine vinegar
1 teaspoon crushed dried tarragon
1 teaspoon dried mustard
½ teaspoon salt
¼ teaspoon dried dillweed
¼ teaspoon sugar
Lettuce leaves
2 hard-boiled eggs, chopped

Arrange beet and cucumber slices in overlapping rows on platter. In a jar combine oil, vinegar, tarragon, mustard, salt, dillweed, and sugar. Shake well. Pour dressing over beets and cucumbers. Refrigerate at least 1 hour. Arrange lettuce around edges of platter and sprinkle chopped egg over top.

Marinated Zucchini Salad _____

Makes 4 to 6 servings

3 cups sliced zucchini
2 medium tomatoes, coarsely chopped
1 cup sliced fresh mushrooms
2 tablespoons thinly sliced green onion
½ cup white wine vinegar
⅓ cup olive oil *or* vegetable oil
1 tablespoon sugar
1 clove garlic, minced
½ teaspoon salt
½ teaspoon dried basil, crushed
Dash of pepper
Lettuce leaves
Shredded mozzarella or Monterey Jack cheese (optional)

Cook zucchini in a small amount of boiling salted water about 3 minutes or until crisp-tender; drain. In a shallow dish combine cooked zucchini, tomatoes, mushrooms, and onion. To make dressing, in a screw-top jar combine vinegar, oil, sugar, garlic, salt, basil, and pepper. Cover and shake well. Pour dressing over zucchini mixture; toss lightly. Cover and chill several hours or overnight, stirring occasionally. To serve, drain zucchini mixture, reserving dressing. Arrange zucchini mixture on lettuce-lined plates. Top with shredded cheese and pass additional dressing, if desired.

Deluxe Potato Salad _____

Makes 6 servings

8 medium-sized new potatoes
1 10½-ounce can bouillon
1 large red onion, finely chopped
12 cherry tomatoes
1 4-ounce can artichoke hearts, drained and sliced
4 hard-boiled eggs, diced
Chopped parsley
Salt and pepper
1 cup mayonnaise

Boil the potatoes in their jackets until tender (about 25 minutes). Drain. When cool, peel and slice. Marinate the potato slices in the bouillon for 1 hour. Put chopped onion into a salad bowl or sealable plastic container. Add tomatoes, artichoke hearts, eggs, and a sprinkle of chopped parsley; salt and pepper to taste. Just before serving, drain the potatoes and add to vegetables. Stir in mayonnaise and serve immediately.

Bean Sprout Salad

Makes 4 servings

¼ **cup olive oil**
2 **tablespoons wine vinegar**
½ **teaspoon salt**
¼ **teaspoon freshly ground pepper**
¼ **cup chopped pimiento**
2 **tablespoons toasted sesame seed**
1 **clove garlic, minced**
3 **cups bean sprouts**

In a jar combine all ingredients except bean sprouts, shake well. Pour over bean sprouts and refrigerate for at least 1 hour.

Creamy Cucumbers

Makes 6 servings

3 **medium cucumbers, thinly sliced**
3 **cups water**
1½ **teaspoons salt**
½ **cup sour cream**
2 **tablespoons cider vinegar**
1 **teaspoon sugar**
½ **teaspoon salt**
½ **teaspoon black pepper**

Layer cucumbers in a medium-sized bowl. Cover with water and 1½ teaspoons salt. Chill. Pour off salted water. Rinse and drain. Blend sour cream, vinegar, and sugar. Fold into cucumbers. Sprinkle with salt and pepper. Chill for several hours before serving.

Lima Bean Salad

Makes 4 to 6 servings

1 **10½-ounce package frozen lima beans**
⅔ **cup chopped green onion**
2 **hard-boiled eggs, chopped**
  Freshly ground black pepper
  Salt
  Parsley, chopped
½ **cup pitted black olives**

Cook lima beans according to package directions until tender; cool. Mix remaining ingredients and combine with beans. Serve with a vinegar and oil dressing. Chill until serving time.

Insalada Rosa, 44;
Lima Bean Salad, this page

Molded Salads

Asparagus-Celery Aspic

Makes 3 servings

3 cups canned asparagus tips, liquid reserved
1 3-ounce package unflavored gelatin
  Chicken *or* canned bouillon
  Salt
  Paprika
2 cups chopped celery
  Mayonnaise

Soften gelatin in 3 tablespoons of asparagus liquid. Heat remaining liquid; stir in gelatin mixture and heat until dissolved. If needed, add bouillon to make 2 cups of liquid. Season with salt and paprika. Pour into 3-cup mold and chill until almost set. Stir in celery and asparagus tips; chill until firm. Unmold and serve with mayonnaise.

Pineapple-Marshmallow Salad

Makes 12 servings

1 3-ounce package lemon gelatin
1 3-ounce package orange gelatin
2 cups boiling water
1½ cups cold water
1 20-ounce can crushed pineapple, juice reserved
2 bananas, diced
1½ to 2 cups miniature marshmallows
2 tablespoons butter *or* margarine
2 tablespoons flour
½ cup sugar
1 large egg, lightly beaten
1 cup whipping cream
1 to 1½ cups shredded sharp Cheddar cheese

Combine gelatins in large mixing bowl; add boiling water. Stir until gelatin dissolves. Stir in cold water and chill until partially set. Add pineapple, bananas, and marshmallows. Turn into a 9 x 13-inch glass pan; chill until set. Melt butter in small saucepan until sizzling; add flour at once. Cook, stirring constantly for 1 minute. Add sugar, egg, and 1 cup of reserved pineapple juice. Cook until thickened. Cool. Whip cream until it holds soft peaks; fold into cooled mixture. Spread over gelatin and sprinkle with cheese.

Rice Salad

Makes 6 servings

4 cups cooked rice
1 cup chopped cooked chicken
½ cup sour cream
½ cup mayonnaise
¼ cup cooked green peas
½ cup diced celery
¼ cup diced green olives
1 teaspoon seasoned salt
Hard-boiled eggs, shelled and sliced
Tomatoes, cut in wedges
Lettuce

Mix together all ingredients except eggs, tomatoes, and lettuce. Gently press rice mixture into a mold. Unmold on a bed of lettuce and garnish with eggs and tomatoes.

Heavenly Cheese Mold

Makes 6 servings

1 envelope unflavored gelatin
¼ cup water
1 cup milk, divided
1½ cups cottage cheese
¼ cup crumbled blue cheese
1 6-ounce can frozen limeade concentrate, thawed
½ cup chopped pecans
½ cup whipping cream, whipped
Salad greens

In a small saucepan sprinkle gelatin over water. Let stand to soften then stir in ½ cup milk. Cook over low heat until gelatin dissolves, stirring constantly. Stir in remaining milk. In mixing bowl beat cheeses until smooth. Stir in gelatin mixture and limeade. Chill until partially set. Fold in pecans and whipped cream. Pour into a 4½-cup ring mold. Chill until firm and unmold on a bed of salad greens.

Strawberry-Pineapple Salad

Makes 4 servings

1 8-ounce package cream cheese, softened
3 tablespoons honey
2 cups strawberries, hulled and crushed
1 cup crushed pineapple, drained

Combine cream cheese and honey in a bowl. Add strawberries and pineapple; blend well. Pour into a freezer tray and freeze 2 hours. Cut into 4 portions. Serve on lettuce leaves and garnish with strawberry slices, if desired.

Nutty Cantaloupe Salad

Makes 6 to 8 servings

1 3-ounce package orange,
  lemon, *or* lime gelatin
  Dash salt
1 cup boiling water
¾ cup cold water
1 teaspoon lemon juice
1 cup diced cantaloupe *or*
  small cantaloupe balls
¼ cup sliced celery
¼ cup finely slivered almonds
1 3-ounce package cream
  cheese
2 tablespoons mayonnaise

Dissolve gelatin and salt in boiling water. Add cold water and lemon juice. Chill half of mixture until very thick. Fold in cantaloupe, celery, and almonds. Pour into a shallow pan or individual molds and chill until set but not firm. Mix cheese and mayonnaise until smooth. Blend in remaining gelatin gradually. Pour over other layer of gelatin and chill until firm. Unmold on lettuce and serve with cream cheese balls, if desired.

Cheesy Apricot Mold

Makes 8 servings

1 3-ounce package lemon
  gelatin
1 cup boiling water
1 can apricots, sliced, one cup
  juice reserved
1½ cups cottage cheese
1 cup whipping cream, whipped
½ cup coarsely chopped walnuts
½ cup maraschino cherries,
  quartered
  Sliced canned apricots,
  optional

In small bowl dissolve gelatin in boiling water. Stir in reserved apricot juice and chill until partially set. Stir in cottage cheese. Fold in whipped cream, nuts, cherries, and apricots. Pour into lightly oiled 1½-quart mold and chill until firm. Unmold and garnish with extra apricot slices, if desired.

Strawberry-Pineapple Salad, 53

Strawberry-Coconut Salad _____

Makes 8 to 10 servings

2 **envelopes unflavored gelatin**
⅓ **cup sugar**
 Dash salt
2 **cups milk**
2 **large eggs, separated**
1 **teaspoon vanilla extract**
½ **teaspoon rum extract**
1 **cup flaked coconut**
1 **cup whipping cream**
1 **pint fresh strawberries, hulled**

Combine gelatin, sugar, and salt in top of double boiler; set over hot but not boiling water. Stir in milk until gelatin is dissolved. Lightly beat egg yolks. Whisk ½ cup of hot mixture into yolks then add back in. Cook in double boiler, stirring constantly until mixture thickens and coats back of spoon. Remove from heat and cool. Stir in extracts and coconut. Beat egg whites until stiff but not dry. Beat whipping cream until soft peaks form. Fold egg whites and whipping cream into coconut mixture. Turn into 6½-cup mold. Chill until firm; unmold onto serving platter. Garnish with strawberries and additional coconut.

Lemon-Lime Cheese Mold _____

Makes 8 servings

1 **20-ounce can crushed pineapple, juice reserved**
1 **3-ounce package lime gelatin**
1 **3-ounce package lemon gelatin**
1½ **cups boiling water**
1 **3-ounce package cream cheese**
1 **cup heavy cream, whipped**

Add enough water to reserved pineapple juice to make 2 cups. Heat to a boil; remove from heat and add lime gelatin. Stir to dissolve. Refrigerate until mixture begins to thicken. Fold in pineapple. Pour into an oiled 7-cup mold and refrigerate until almost firm. Dissolve lemon gelatin in boiling water. Refrigerate until thickened. Blend in cream cheese and beat until fluffy. Fold in cream; pour over lime layer. Refrigerate until firm. Unmold and garnish with greens and assorted fruits.

Sunny Side Salad

Makes 6 servings

1 3-ounce package lemon *or* orange-pineapple gelatin
½ teaspoon salt
1½ cups boiling water
1 can crushed pineapple
1 tablespoon lemon juice
1 cup coarsely grated carrots
⅓ cup chopped pecans

Dissolve gelatin and salt in boiling water. Add undrained pineapple and lemon juice. Chill until very thick. Fold in carrots and pecans, and pour into individual molds or a 1-quart mold. Chill until firm. Unmold and garnish with additional pineapple, if desired.

Purple Berry Salad

Makes 8 servings

2 3-ounce packages strawberry gelatin
1 cup boiling water
1 8-ounce can crushed pineapple, juice reserved
1 8-ounce can blueberries in heavy syrup, syrup reserved
1 banana, sliced
1 cup prepared whipped topping
½ cup chopped nuts

Dissolve gelatin in boiling water. Add pineapple with juice, blueberries with syrup, and banana. Refrigerate until thick. Fold in whipped topping and nuts and serve.

Eggnog Salad

Makes 8 servings

2 envelopes unflavored gelatin
1 16-ounce can fruit cocktail, drained, juice reserved
1 11-ounce can mandarin oranges, drained
1 cup flaked coconut
2½ cups dairy eggnog
   Dash nutmeg
½ cup halved maraschino cherries

Soften gelatin in fruit cocktail juice. Heat in double boiler until gelatin is completely dissolved. Combine with remaining ingredients and pour into a 5-cup mold. Refrigerate until firm.

Dressings

Herbed Yogurt Dressing

Makes 2½ cups

¾ cup mayonnaise
¾ cup plain yogurt
1 clove garlic, minced
2 tablespoons chopped onion
½ cup chopped parsley
¼ cup minced fresh dill
¼ teaspoon dried tarragon
3 tablespoons cider vinegar

Place ingredients in blender. Cover and blend until smooth. Chill until serving time.

Green Goddess Dressing

Makes 2 cups

1 8-ounce container plain yogurt
1 cup mayonnaise
2 tablespoons lemon juice
2 tablespoons chopped scallion
2 tablespoons finely chopped parsley
½ teaspoon Worcestershire sauce
¼ teaspoon garlic salt
Salt and pepper

Combine all ingredients in bowl. Chill for 1 hour before serving. Pour over tossed salads.

Roquefort Dressing _____

Makes 3½ cups

2 cups mayonnaise
1 cup sour cream
½ cup wine vinegar
3 tablespoons anchovy paste
2 tablespoons lemon juice
2 cloves garlic, minced
¼ pound Roquefort cheese

In medium mixing bowl combine mayonnaise, sour cream, vinegar, anchovy paste, lemon juice, and garlic. Mix well. Crumble cheese into dressing; mix lightly. Cover and chill before serving on tossed salads.

Italian Dressing _____

Makes 2½ cups

¾ cup red wine vinegar
Juice of one lemon
1 teaspoon salt
½ teaspoon sugar
½ teaspoon dry mustard
1½ teaspoons Worcestershire sauce
1 large clove garlic, minced
½ cup vegetable oil
½ cup olive oil

Combine all ingredients and mix well. Chill several hours. Pour over tossed salads.

Celery-Dill Dressing _____

Makes 1 cup

½ cup plain yogurt
3 tablespoons mayonnaise
Milk
Celery salt
Dillweed

Mix together yogurt and mayonnaise. Thin with milk. Season to taste with celery salt and dillweed.

Minty Lime Dressing

Makes 1¼ cups

1 8-ounce container plain yogurt
3 tablespoons freshly squeezed and strained lime juice
1½ tablespoons green creme de menthe liqueur

Combine all ingredients and blend thoroughly. Cover and chill. Serve on fruit salads.

Caper-Mustard Dressing

Makes 2½ cups

2 8-ounce containers plain yogurt
2 tablespoons capers
2 tablespoons prepared mustard
4 scallions, finely chopped
1 teaspon dried dillweed
Salt and pepper to taste

Blend all ingredients in a bowl. Chill before serving with tossed salads. Can also be used as sauce for fish or cold beef.

Creamy Tarragon Dressing

Makes 1 cup

1 egg yolk
2 teaspoons spicy mustard
1 teaspoon red wine vinegar
¾ cup vegetable oil
1 teaspoon tarragon
Salt and pepper to taste

Whisk egg yolk for 1 minute. Add mustard and vinegar and continue beating for another minute. Slowly add oil while beating; blend well. Stir in tarragon, salt, and pepper. Chill until serving time.

Seafood Salad Dressing

Makes 1¾ cups

1 **cup mayonnaise**
1½ **tablespoons Dijon-style mustard**
¼ **teaspoon dried tarragon**
1 **tablespoon red wine vinegar**
1 **tablespoon water** *or* **milk**
Salt and pepper to taste

Combine all ingredients in blender. Blend until smooth.

Honey-Almond Dressing

Makes 2 cups

½ **cup mayonnaise**
½ **cup honey**
¼ **cup slivered almonds**
¼ **teaspoon almond extract**
1 **8-ounce container plain yogurt**

Mix together first four ingredients. Fold in yogurt. Chill. Serve with fruit salads.

Poppy Seed Dressing

Makes 2 cups

¼ **cup honey**
¼ **cup cider vinegar**
2 **tablespoons prepared mustard**
3 **tablespoons poppy seed**
1 **small onion, minced**
¼ **teaspoon salt**
¾ **cup vegetable oil**

Combine all ingredients in a screw-top jar. Shake to mix. Chill until serving time. Pour over tossed salads.

Caper-Mustard Dressing, 61;
Green Goddess Dressing, 59;
Minty Lime Dressing, 61;
Honey-Almond Dressing, this page

Index

DRESSINGS

Caper-Mustard Dressing, 61
Celery-Dill Dressing, 60
Creamy Tarragon Dressing, 61
Green Goddess Dressing, 59
Herbed Yogurt Dressing, 59
Honey-Almond Dressing, 62
Italian Dressing, 60
Minty Lime Dressing, 61
Poppy Seed Dressing, 62
Roquefort Dressing, 60
Seafood Salad Dressing, 62

FANCY FRUIT SALADS

Ambrosia, 4
Cheese-Stuffed Pears, 11
Frozen Fantasy, 5
Fruit and Cheese Salad, 5
Grape Cup, 4
Guacamole Salad, 9
Homemade Applesauce, 4
Honey-Lime Pineapple Salad, 8
Melon Madness, 5
Nutty Fruit Slaw, 9
Old-Fashioned Waldorf Salad, 8
Overnight Fruit Salad, 11
Pineapple-Pecan Salad, 6
Tropical Waldorf Salad, 6

MAIN DISH SALADS

Beef and Walnut Salad Spread, 24
Chicken Salad Spread, 24
East-West Pork Salad, 31
Five Bean Salad, 29
Ham Salad Spread, 24
Hot German Potato Salad, 27
Kona Ham Hawaiian, 29
Layered Chef's Salad, 25
Mexican Salad, 25

Oriental Chicken Salad, 32
Reuben Salad, 28
Shanghai Salad, 31
Spring Spinach Salad, 28
Stuffed Pepper Salad, 27
Tarragon Chicken Salad, 32

MOLDED SALADS

Asparagus-Celery Aspic, 52
Cheesy Apricot Mold, 55
Eggnog Salad, 57
Heavenly Cheese Mold, 53
Lemon-Lime Cheese Mold, 56
Nutty Cantaloupe Salad, 55
Pineapple-Marshmallow Salad, 52
Purple Berry Salad, 57
Rice Salad, 53
Strawberry-Coconut Salad, 56
Strawberry-Pineapple Salad, 53
Sunny Side Salad, 57

PASTA PLEASERS

Cool Vegetable Pasta Salad, 22
Fruity Macaroni, 22
Italian Macaroni Salad, 19
Macaroni Chicken Salad, 20
Nectarine Pork Pasta, 21
Pasta Primavera, 20
Shell Salad, 19
Ziti Tomato Mix, 21

SEAFOOD SPECIALS

Crabmeat Salad, 15
Crunchy Salmon Salad Spread, 13
Curried Shrimp Salad, 15
Herring and Beets, 12
Salade Nicoise, 16
Shrimp and Scallop Salad, 17
South Sea Salad, 17

Spicy Salad Baskets, 13
Tuna Salad, 16
Tuna Tater Salad, 12

TEMPTING TOSSES

Avocado and Tomato Salad, 41
Caesar Salad, 33
California Salad, 37
Cracked Wheat Salad, 35
Cucumber Salad, 40
Green and White Asparagus Salad, 37
Hearts of Palm Salad, 41
Mushroom Salad, 36
Nutty Vegetable Salad, 42
Orange-Almond Salad, 42
Pineapple-Spinach Salad, 39
South-of-the-Border Salad, 36
Spinach-Cabbage Salad, 35
Sunny Salsa Salad, 39
Tomato-Pepper Shake, 37
Vinaigrette Coleslaw, 40
Watercress Toss, 33

ZESTY MARINADES

Antipasto Salad, 45
Bean Sprout Salad, 51
Beet and Cucumber Salad, 48
Carrot and Raisin Salad, 46
Cauliflower Salad, 45
Corn Relish, 46
Creamy Cucumbers, 51
Deluxe Potato Salad, 49
Deviled Egg Salad, 48
Insalada Rosa, 44
Lima Bean Salad, 51
Marinated Onion Salad, 46
Marinated Zucchini Salad, 49
Three Bean Salad, 44